ADVICE FROM THE
PENGUINS

I0539902

Dr. Muriel
McClellan

ADVICE FROM THE PENGUINS

Copyright © 2025 **Dr. Muriel S. McClellan**

ISBN (Paperback): 979-8-89672-203-8
ISBN (Hardback): 979-8-89672-205-2
ISBN (Ebook): 979-8-89672-204-5

All rights reserved. No part of this book may be used or reproduced by any means, graphic, electronic, or mechanical, including photocopying, recording, taping or by information storage and retrieval system without the written permission of the author except in the case of brief quotations embodied in critical articles and reviews.

Because of the dynamic nature of the Internet, any web addresses or links contained in this book may have changed since publication and may no longer be valid. The views expressed in the work are solely those of the author and do not necessarily reflect the views of the publisher, and the publisher hereby disclaims any responsibility for them.

Printed in the United States of America.

PROMINENT
BOOKS
EDGE

5830 E 2nd St, Ste 7000 #9983
Casper, WY 82609
USA

About the Author

Dr. McClellan received her Ph.D. from Arizona State University in counseling psychology and her master's degree from UCLA. She completed post doctoral training in family therapy and established a successful private practice as a psychologist for over 35 years in the Phoenix Arizona area. She served in leadership positions and a number of community boards and committees.

While Dr. McClellan enjoyed her private practice, she was always looking for new ideas and inspiration. Her office looked out onto a lake that was inhabited with various migrating ducks. Between sessions she would gaze out of the window and long for more time in nature. That is when she began taking classes with Arizona Highways and attended a workshop on photographing hummingbirds. After that powerful introduction, she was hooked and began studying with distinguished wildlife photographers around the world.

One workshop was to South Georgia in the Southern Ocean to photograph enormous king penguin colonies such as St. Andrews Bay and Salisbury Plain. Dr. McClellan continued onto the Antarctica to discover even more types of penguins in beautiful settings. This experience was a photographer's dream and led to the vision for Advice of the Penguins.

On any adventure, bring those along
who can add value to the experience.

When you are really challenged...consider taking a leap of faith.

It is important to always stay curious.

Penguins always think that two heads are better than none.

That is…two heads are better than one.

Having a bad day?
Keep it in perspective...
so have others.

When you have an itch, scratch it.

If you have a very challenging project…

don't procrastinate, dive right in!

It takes a village to raise a penguin.

If you think your hat might blow off, penguins suggest a chin strap.

Listen when someone says you need a bath.

If you think the beaches are crowded in California…

appreciate what you have and don't move to the Southern Ocean.

When you meet up with a bully…

just walk on by and don't become bait.

If you meet a girl taller than you, just find a rock.

Think outside the box. You don't have to go the same direction as everyone else.

Know how to take a bow after a job well done.

A really good friend will have your back.

Appreciate others who are different than you.

Leadership really matters.

Be careful about who you follow!

If you are pleased, let the whole world know about it.

Always consider the other's point of view.

If you drop the ball…

pick it up and move on.

Resting is very important. Find a comfortable place for you head.

Do your happy dance as often as possible.

But the best advice…
relationships are everything!

www.ingramcontent.com/pod-product-compliance
Lightning Source LLC
Chambersburg PA
CBRC090829120626
46547CB00008B/636